PowerKiDS
Readers
SEA FRIENDS
LOS AMIGOS DEL MAR

HARP SEALS
LAS FOCAS DE GROENLANDIA

SAM DRUMLIN
TRADUCCIÓN AL ESPAÑOL: EDUARDO ALAMÁN

PowerKiDS
press™

New York

Published in 2013 by The Rosen Publishing Group, Inc.
29 East 21st Street, New York, NY 10010

First Edition

Editor: Amelie von Zumbusch
Book Design: Liz Gloor and Colleen Bialecki   Traducción al español: Eduardo Alamán

Photo Credits: Cover John Giustina/Taxi/Getty Images; p. 5 Florida Stock/Shutterstock.com; p. 7 Hiroyuki Matsumoto/Photographer's Choice/Getty Images; p. 9 iStockphoto.com/Thinkstock; p. 11 Vladimir Melnik/Shutterstock.com; p. 13 Ralph Lee Hopkins/National Geographic/Getty Images; pp. 15, 23 Jupiter Images/Photos.com/Thinkstock; p. 17 © Minden Pictures/Superstock; p. 19 AleksandrN/Shutterstock.com; p. 21 Tom Brakefield/Stockbyte/Thinkstock.

Library of Congress Cataloging-in-Publication Data

Drumlin, Sam.
 [Harp seal. English & Spanish]
 Harp seals = Las focas de Groenlandia / by Sam Drumlin ; translated by Eduardo Alamán. — 1st ed.
   p. cm. — (Powerkids readers: sea friends = Los amigos del mar)
 Includes index.
 ISBN 978-1-4488-9973-9 (library binding)
 1. Harp seal—Juvenile literature. I. Title. II. Title: Focas de Groenlandia.
 QL737.P64D7818 2013
 599.79'29—dc23
                                          2012024549

Web Sites: Due to the changing nature of Internet links, PowerKids Press has developed an online list of Web sites related to the subject of this book. This site is updated regularly. Please use this link to access the list: www.powerkidslinks.com/pkrsf/hseal/

Manufactured in the United States of America

CPSIA Compliance Information: Batch #W13PK3: For Further Information contact Rosen Publishing, New York, New York at 1-800-237-9932

CONTENTS

CONTENIDO

Harp seals are cute!

¡Las focas de Groenlandia son muy lindas!

5

They live in the sea.

_____

Viven en el océano.

Babies are **pups**.

Los bebés son **cachorros**.

They are soft.

Son muy suaves.

They are born on **ice floes**.

Nacen en **témpanos de hielo**.

Pups nurse for about
two weeks.

_____

Los cachorros se amamantan
durante unas dos semanas.

In time, pups grow new **coats**.

Con el tiempo, los cachorros tienen nuevo **pelaje**.

They learn to swim.

Los cachorros aprenden
a nadar.

Fish are their main food.

Los peces son su principal alimento.

They grow new coats
each year.

Cada año les crece un
nuevo pelaje.

WORDS TO KNOW / PALABRAS QUE DEBES SABER

coat
(el) pelaje

ice floes
(los) témpanos
de hielo

pup
(el) cachorro

INDEX

ÍNDICE